WHAT WILL YOU DO FOR PEACE?

Impact of 9/11 on New York City Youth

Introduction by Faith Ringgold

InterRelations Collaborative, Inc.

INTRODUCTION

Time stood still on September 11, 2001 as we watched in disbelief. On that sorrowful Tuesday morning we openly grieved for thousands of people. Life is very different for all of us in this new post 9/11 America.

When I was shown the layout for a new book titled, *What Will You Do For Peace? Impact of 9/11 on New York City Youth*, my heart filled with joy. What a beautiful collaboration, a perfect response from New York City's young people, aged 11 to 19. This gracefully poetic account of that frightening day in their young lives is a gift of sensitivity and love. I was amazed at their generosity of spirit. I found the paintings and expressive verse in this book deeply inspiring.

I don't know if I will ever see a world at peace. What I do know is the pursuit of peace requires people with a highly evolved, creative mind and the open heart of the young. So let us all find the courage to believe in peace. And maybe someday there will be a cry for peace that will resound around the world. Until then let us champion the youth of New York City who have raised an important question. It is simple and clear. Each one of us must answer the question with an open heart:

What Will YOU Do For Peace?

Faith Ringgold
September 11, 2004

September 11th. It was a school day.
I was in social studies.
The classrooms were very quiet.
I started to notice that people were being called to go home.
Parents started coming in to get their children.
We didn't know what was going on.

I saw my fifth grade teacher crying so I figured something happened.
My whole class was confused.
Then they called my name and said I'm going home.
My mom picked me up.
I left school heading to the bus and found it wasn't running.
I met my mother and she was going crazy because she was trying to find me.

*I asked my mom what happened
and she looked worried.*

*They had hijacked planes
and were crashing the Twin Towers.
A plane with people in it
had crashed in the Twin Towers.*

It got worse when the World Trade Center collapsed and killed thousands of people.
My mom's best friend died and I started to cry.

I thought I would never see my grandmother again.
Around the same time the Towers were hit
My grandmother usually takes her lunch break
And enters the building to see a friend.
Luckily she had the day off.

My aunt thought one of her brothers
Was in there so she began to cry.
But thank God her brother called her
To tell her that he was OK.

I wasn't allowed to go home because my school was so close.
I saw the whole thing from the dramatic plane crashes to the falling towers.

When I got home, when I turned on the TV,
All I see was news on every channel.
See airplanes crashing into the World Trade Center,
See people flying out the windows.
I was praying for the people who died,
I thought about them.

We were glued to the TV.
When we heard a plane crashed into the Pentagon,
We started to cry.
I will never forget my mom's face.
It will live like thorns in my heart.

I was thinking, "Can we leave the state
And go somewhere else for the time being?"
But they said on the news,
No one can leave New York City.
You can only come in.
So there was nothing you could do.

The day of September 11th was one of the worst days of my life.
Many people suffered that day.
It made me feel sad for all the families who lost
A dad, mom, an uncle, grandmother, any family member.
I just never actually suspected anything like this could happen.

The tragedy of 9/11 will never be forgotten
No matter where you're from.
I was very sad because there were
Too many people who died for no reason.
That very moment I started to think of the future.
I hope that in the future, the kids now
Will make a better world for everybody else.

I wondered, "Was America ever going to be the same?"
This made me think about peace.

P is for PEOPLE united as one.
E is for EVERYONE treated equally.
A is for AROUND THE WORLD people are going to make peace.
C is for COUNTRIES unite as brothers and sisters.
E is for EVERYONE will achieve this goal one day.

People united as 1. EveryOne treated equally. Around the World People are going to make peace. Countries Unite as brothers and sisters. EVeryone Will achieve this goal 1 day !!!!!

We made a peace poster.
It says: "What Will U Do 4 Peace?"
Notice the "peace" letters are broken in parts now.
We as people have to fix them together.

We should all gather together.

You should never feel left out.
You are a piece of a puzzle
and without you
The whole picture can't be seen.

Communicate and interact.

Peacemakers are powerful people.

"What will <u>YOU</u> do for peace?"

CONTRIBUTORS

Published by
InterRelations Collaborative, Inc.
PO Box 6280
Hamden, CT 06517

ISBN 0-9761753-0-4

Printed by
RJ Communications, LLC
51 East 42nd Street, Suite 1202
New York, NY 10017

Book Design: BudgetBookDesign.com

Photography by Matthew Bradbury

Printed in the United States

We are exceedingly grateful to the celebrated artist, Faith Ringgold, for her invaluable guidance throughout the creative process. We thank her for selecting the youth artwork and for graciously writing the introduction.

We acknowledge with appreciation our community associates for bringing together outstanding New York City youth to document their experiences on 9/11: Ana Ofelia Rodriguez and Rafaela Capellan of Broadway Housing Communities; Oscar Gee of Chinese American Planning Council; Barry O'Connor of Forest Hills Community House; Johanny Cepeda and Roseann Gomez of Grand Street Settlement House; Stephanie Pinder and Roxy McCarroll of Lincoln Square Neighborhood Center; Elizabeth Yeampierre of the United Puerto Rican Organization of Sunset Park; Songyun Kang and Won Kang of YWCA Flushing Center, and Alexie Torres-Fleming of Youth Ministries for Peace and Justice.

The InterRelations Collaborative gratefully acknowledges the generous support of the United Way of New York City.